PSALM SONGS 3

Ordinary Time

Edited by David Ogden and Alan Smith

Augsburg Fortress
PUBLISHERS

Augsburg Fortress Publishers
PO Box 1209
Minneapolis, MN 55440-1209
USA

Library of Congress Cataloging-in-Publication Data
Applied for.

ISBN 0-8006-5772-1

Psalm Songs 1	ISBN 0-8006-5770-5
Psalm Songs 2	ISBN 0-8006-5771-3
Psalm Songs set	ISBN 0-8006-5773-X

Music and text typeset by Alan and Dave Smith

Printed and bound in Great Britain by Redwood Books, Trowbridge, Wiltshire

Contents

Dedicated to the memory of
Geoffrey Boulton Smith

Introduction

The idea for these three volumes of *Psalm Songs* was first conceived in 1994 by Geoffrey Boulton Smith, then Director of Music for the Roman Catholic Diocese of Portsmouth. Geoffrey had spent much of his life composing and encouraging others to compose music for the liturgy, especially since the reforms of the Second Vatican Council. After his untimely death in 1996 we undertook to complete the project.

The original plan was to provide a responsorial song setting of the psalm for each of the Sundays and principal feast days in both the Roman Lectionary and the Revised Common Lectionary (as adopted by the Church of England in *Calendar, Lectionary and Collects*). In the event it proved impossible to find suitable settings of every one of these psalms, but all the commonly used texts have been included. We have used the Hebrew psalm numbers rather than those in the Greek Septuagint. So, for example, 'The Lord is my shepherd' appears as the twenty-third psalm, and not as the twenty-second.

The psalms are the prayer book of the Bible – the human expression of dialogue between the people of Israel and their God. From the earliest times, a singer was engaged in the synagogues to minister at the scrolls and to lead the psalm singing. They would stand before the ark of the scrolls and intone the liturgy – a leader of prayer on behalf of the assembly. The psalm is a personal response to the Word of God and so today is most suitably placed after the first reading in a eucharistic celebration. In recent years psalm singing has been given fresh impetus by the use of responsorial settings which give scope for solo cantors and choirs, and for the congregation to engage in dialogue with them. *Psalm Songs* brings together 79 such settings, all but two of which have a congregational refrain. (The two exceptions may be sung in their entirety by the congregation.)

There are various ways in which you can help and encourage your congregation to take a full and active part in the singing of these psalms:

- duplicate the congregational refrains which are printed at the back of the books onto your service sheet.
- arrange for a cantor to stand in full view of the people and discreetly indicate when they should sing.
- do not overwhelm your congregation with new material every Sunday. The *common psalms* in the Roman Lectionary will often do duty for several consecutive weeks.
- a short congregational practice before the celebration begins will instil confidence – but don't annoy your people by having one every Sunday.

Some of these settings may be too long or too elaborate for your needs; if so, save them for that 'big occasion' and use a simpler tone or chant setting. This is especially true of the Liturgy of the Word / Ministry of the Word at the principal service on Sundays, where the psalm should reflect on the readings rather than dominate. Some of these settings might be more appropriate at other times in the service: as the entrance song, during communion or as a conclusion to the celebration. Again, those congregations that communally celebrate the Prayer of the Church (in whatever form) will find much here to aid their worship.

Many of the pieces in *Psalm Songs* are published here for the first time. They have all been composed by musicians working in churches today, and they encompass a wide range of contemporary musical styles. In performance the songs should have a sense of growth, with the optional parts for choir and instruments being used to colour or embellish the vocal parts rather than providing a wash of sound, and then only after the congregation can confidently sing the refrain.

We would like to express our thanks to those who have helped us see Geoffrey Boulton Smith's vision through to its fulfilment: the members of the Composers' Group of the Society of Saint Gregory (many of whom are represented in these pages), our wives Lucy and Pauline, and above all Ruth McCurry from Cassell for her commitment, guidance and enthusiasm for this project.

We hope that *Psalm Songs* will find a home in your church and help to make the Word of God live in the hearts of your congregation.

David Ogden & Alan Smith

Canticle Of Daniel

Daniel 3:52-56

Christopher Walker

VERSES: *Cantor/Choir*

1. You are blest   Lord God!   You are blest for your   name is most   glo - rious.
2. You are blest   Lord God!   You are blest in your   tem - ple of   glo - ry.
3. You are blest   Lord God!   You are blest on the   throne of your   pow - er.
4. You are blest   Lord God!   You are blest as you   gaze in the   depths._____
5. You are blest   Lord God!   You are blest in the   height of the   heav - ens.

1. You are blest   Lord God!   You are blest for your   name is most   glo - rious.
2. You are blest   Lord God!   You are blest in your   tem - ple of   glo - ry.
3. You are blest   Lord God!   You are blest on the   throne of your   pow - er.
4. You are blest   Lord God!   You are blest as you   gaze in the   depths._____
5. You are blest   Lord God!   You are blest in the   height of the   heav - ens.

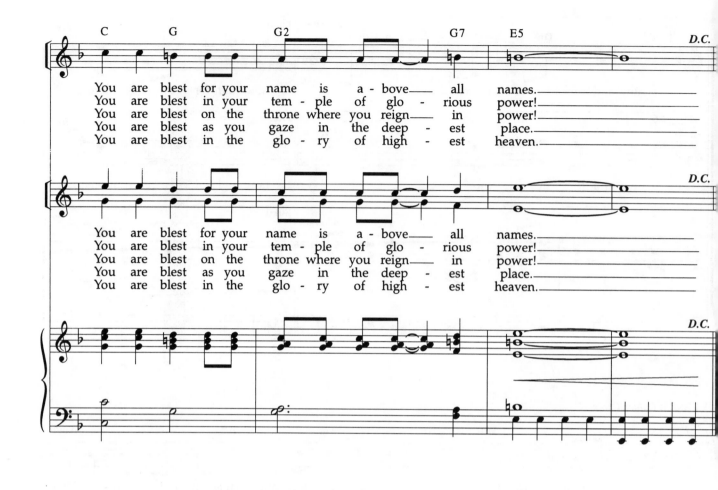

You are blest for your name is a - bove____ all names.____
You are blest in your tem - ple of glo - rious power!____
You are blest on the throne where you reign____ in power!____
You are blest as you gaze in the deep - est place.____
You are blest in the glo - ry of high - est heaven.____

You are blest for your name is a - bove____ all names.____
You are blest in your tem - ple of glo - rious power!____
You are blest on the throne where you reign____ in power!____
You are blest as you gaze in the deep - est place.____
You are blest in the glo - ry of high - est heaven.____

You Are A Priest For Ever

Psalm 110

Geoffrey Boulton Smith

You are a priest for ev - er,____ a priest like Mel - chiz - e - dek of old. old. old.

1. The Lord's rev - e - la - tion to my Mas - ter: "Sit on my

2. The Lord will send from Zi - on your scep - tre of

3. A prince from the day of your birth on the ho - ly

4. The Lord has sworn an oath he will not change. "You are a priest for

right: I will put your foes be - neath your feet."

power: rule in the midst of all your foes.

moun - tains; from the womb be - fore the day - break I be - got you.

ev - er, a priest like Mel - chiz - e - dek of old."

Your Name Is Praised

for David and Lucy

Psalm 8

Patrick Geary

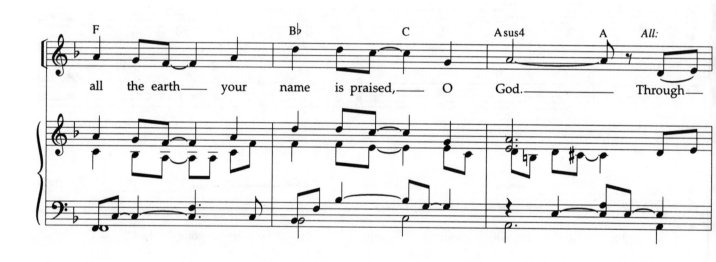

VERSE 1: *Cantor*

A-bove the hea-vens your maj-es-ty is sung by chil-dren and babes. Be-

fore you your foes are re - duced to si - lence.

VERSE 2: *Cantor*

When I look at— the work of your hands,— the moon and stars which you have

11

made,_____ I won-der, I won-der at___ your care for___ your people.

VERSE 3: *Unaccompanied choir (or accompanied cantor, singing top line)*

Soprano
Alto

With glo - ry and hon - our you crown_____

Tenor
Bass

us, giv - ing us pow'r o - ver all you have made._____

FINAL REFRAIN: *All*

Through all the earth, through all the earth your name is praised, O God. Through all the earth, through all the earth your name is praised, O God.

13

Here I Am

Psalm 25

David Ogden

here I am, I come to do your will, Lord, your love is in my

here I am, Lord, here I am, Lord, your love is in my

heart. heart. 2. Re – heart.
  3. The

heart. heart. heart.

15

VERSES: *Cantor*

1. Lord, make me know your ways. Lord, mem-ber your mer-cy, Lord, and the love you have Lord is good and up-right. He shows the path to

teach me your paths. Make me walk in your truth, and shown from of old. In your love re- those who stray, he guides the hum-ble in the

16

teach   me: for   you   are   God my sav - iour._____

mem - ber   me,   be - cause   of your   good - ness, O   Lord._____

right   path;   he   teach - es   his way____ to   the   poor._____

O Lord, Be My Help

Psalm 71

David Ogden

VERSES: *Cantor/Choir*

1. It is you, O Lord, who will res-cue me, who will hear my voice when I call._____ It is you, O Lord, who will free me from sin, and_____
2. It is you, O Lord, who will com-fort me, who will shel-ter me with_____ care._____ It is you, O Lord, who will show me the truth and_____
3. All my life you've walked close_____ by my side, a help and joy from_____ birth._____ My_____ lips shall speak of your might-y deeds, and your

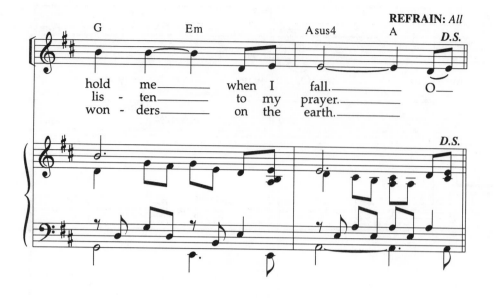

				REFRAIN: *All*
hold me	when I fall.	O		
lis - ten	to my prayer.			
won - ders	on the earth.			

Laudate Dominum

Psalm 117

Jacques Berthier

Lau - da - te Do - mi-num, lau - da - te Do - mi-num om - nes

VERSES: *Cantor*

Praise — the Lord, all you na-tions, praise God all you — peo-ples. Al - le -

lu - ia. Strong is God's love and mer-cy, al - ways faith-ful for ev - er. Al - le - lu -

ia. Al-le - lu - ia, al-le - lu - ia. Let ev-'ry-thing liv-ing give praise to the

Lord. Al-le - lu - ia, al-le - lu - ia. Let ev-'ry-thing liv-ing give praise to the Lord.

Good People Are A Light

Psalm 112

Paul Inwood

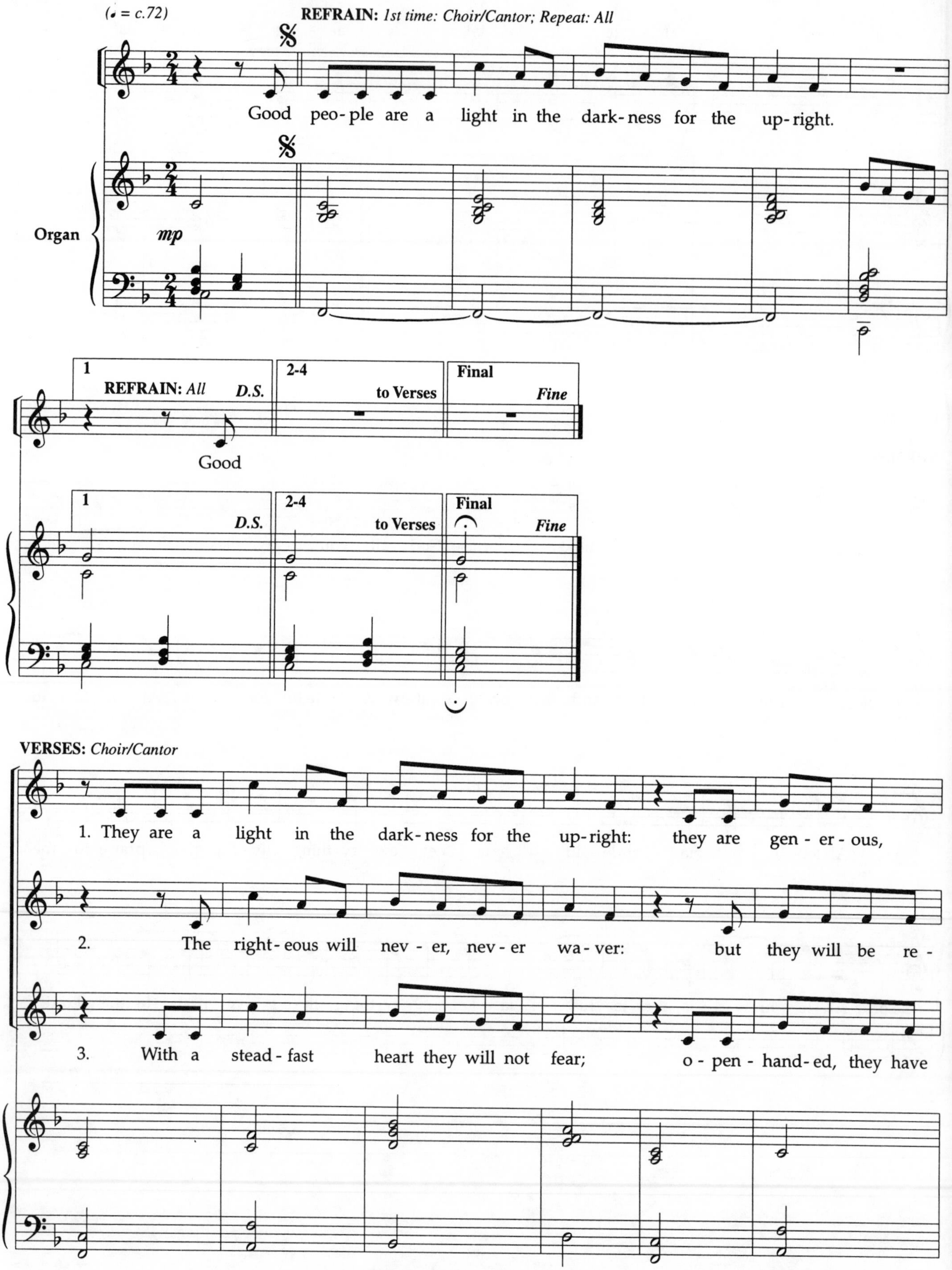

mer - ci - ful and just. Good peo - ple take pit - y and lend, they are

mem - bered for ev - er. They have no fear of e - vil news; with a

giv - en to the poor; their jus - tice en - dures___ for ev - er. Their

REFRAIN: *All* **D.S.**

ho - nest in all their deal - ings. Good

REFRAIN: *All* **D.S.**

firm heart they trust in the Lord. Good

REFRAIN: *All* **D.S.**

heads will be raised in glo - ry. Good

D.S.

Praise The Lord

Psalm 147

Christopher Polyblank

VERSE 1: *Cantor*

1. Al - le - lu - ia! Praise the Lord, for he is good; sing to our

God, for he is lov - ing: to him our praise is due.

Slower

D.S.

VERSE 2: *Cantor/Choir* *

2. The Lord builds up Je - ru - sa - lem and brings back Is - rael's ex - iles, he

he

* In verses 2 and 3, the cantor's first note overlaps the end of the Refrain.

25

heals the bro- ken heart- ed, he binds up all their wounds. He fix-es the num- ber of the

heals the bro- ken heart- ed,

Slower   D.S.

stars; he calls each one by its name.

Slower   D.S.

VERSE 3: *Cantor/Choir*

3. Our Lord is great and al-might-y; his wis-dom can nev-er be meas-ured. The

f 3. Our Lord is great and al-might-y; his wis-dom can nev-er be meas-ured.

Lord rais-es the low-ly; he hum-bles the wick-ed to the earth.

Ah_____ Ah_____

In The Presence Of The Angels

Psalm 138

Paul Inwood

Smoothly (♩ = c.50)

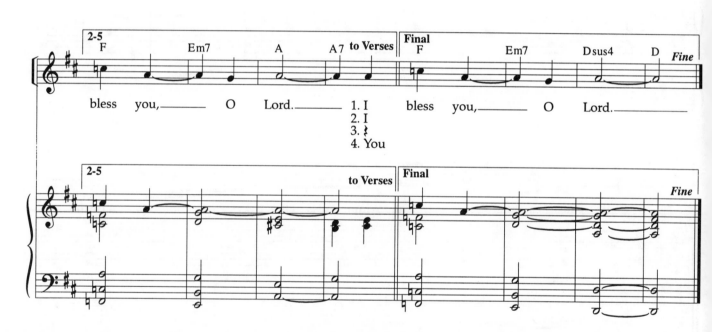

1. thank you, Lord, with all my heart, you have heard the
2. thank you for your faith - ful - ness and love_____ which ex - cel
3. All earth's kings shall thank you_____ when they hear the
4. stretch out your hand and save me,_____ your hand will do

words of my mouth. I will bless you in the pres - ence of the an - gels.
all we ev - er knew of you. On the day I called, you an - swered;
words of your mouth. They shall sing of the Lord's ways:
all things for me. Your love, O Lord, is e - ter - nal,

I will a - dore be - fore your ho - ly tem - ple.

you in - creased the strength of my soul.

"How great is the glo - ry of the Lord!"

dis - card not the work of your hands.

Teach Me, O God

Psalm 119

Christopher Walker

VERSES: *Cantor/Choir*

1. Hap - py are they whose life is blame - less,_____ who fol - low God's
2. It is your will we keep your pre - cepts,_____ o - bey - ing them
3. Bless me, your serv - ant, in your kind - ness,_____ o - bey - ing your
4. Teach me the way that I must fol - low,_____ that I will be

It Is Good To Give Thanks

Psalm 92

Stephen Dean

INTRO: (♩ = c.120)

Keyboard

REFRAIN: *1st time: Cantor; Repeat: All*

It is good to give thanks— to the Lord; to pro - claim your love, O Most High!

VERSE 1: *Cantor*

1. It is good to give thanks— to the Lord, to make mu-sic to your name, O Most

High, to pro - claim your love— in the morn-ing

and your truth in the watch-es of the night.

REFRAIN: *All*

It is good to give thanks— to the Lord; to pro-claim your love, O Most High!

VERSE 2: *Cantor*

2. They will flour-ish, the just,— like the palm-tree, like a Leb-a-non ce - dar grow

tall; in the Lord's own house— they are plant-ed,

in the courts of our God— they will stand.

REFRAIN: *All*

It is good to give thanks— to the Lord; to pro-claim your love, O Most High!

VERSE 3: *Cantor*

3. Still bear-ing fruit when they are old; still full of

sap, still green; to pro-claim that the Lord—— is just.

In him, my rock,— there is no wrong.

FINAL REFRAIN: *All*

It is good to give thanks— to the Lord; to pro - claim your love, O Most High!

rit.

Fine

p

I Will Show God's Salvation

Psalm 50

Stephen Dean

spo-ken and sum-moned the earth, from the ris-ing of the sun to its set-ting.

"I find no fault with your sac-ri-fi-ces, your of-fer-ings are al-ways be-fore me."

VERSE 2: *Cantor*

2. "Were I hun-gry, I would not tell you, for I own the world and all it holds.

Do you think I eat the flesh of bulls, or drink the blood of goats?"

39

VERSE 3: *Cantor*

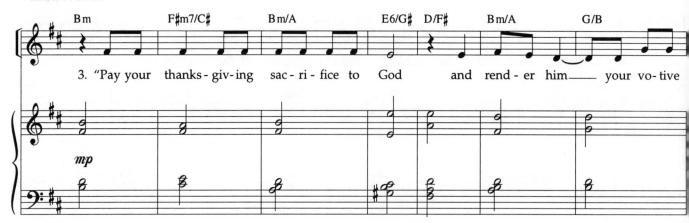

3. "Pay your thanks-giv-ing sac-ri-fice to God and rend-er him___ your vo-tive

of-fer-ings. Call on me in the day of dis-tress. I will free you and

you shall___ hon-our me."

De Profundis Blues

Psalm 130

Paul Wellicome

REFRAIN: *1st time: Cantor/Choir; Repeat: All*

The Lord will bring mer-cy and grant us full par-don. The Lord gives us free-dom from our sins.

All: The sins.

sins.

sound_____ of my voice raised_____ up plead - ing._____ From the

cause_____ you for - give we stand in awe of you._____ From the

sen - tries for dawn, I watch for you, my Lord._____ From the

Lord_____ will free Is - rael from all its sin._____ From the

depths_____ I call_____ to you. The_____

depths_____ I call_____ to you. The_____

depths_____ I call_____ to you. The_____

depths_____ I call_____ to you. The_____

Your Love Is Finer Than Life

Psalm 63

Marty Haugen

VERSE 1: *Cantor/Choir*

1. As a dry and wea-ry des-ert land, so my soul is thirst-ing for my God, and my flesh is faint for the God I seek, for your love is more to me than life.

VERSE 2: *Cantor/Choir*

2. I think of you when at night I rest, I re-flect up-on your stead-fast love. I will

cling to you, Oh Lord my God, in the sha-dow of your wings I sing.

VERSE 3: *Cantor/Choir*

3. I will bless your name all the days I live, I will raise my hands and call on you. My

joy-ful lips shall sing your praise, you a-lone have filled my hun-gry soul.

FINAL REFRAIN: *All*

Our Eyes Are On The Lord

Psalm 123

Philip Duffy

VERSES: *Cantor*

1. To you have I lift-ed up my eyes,

2. Like the eyes, the eyes of a serv-ant on the

3. Have mer-cy, have mer-cy on us, Lord. We are

mp

Ah... Ah...

mp

Solo top line in verses 1 & 3

p

solo

(play top line in verses 1 & 3 only)

49

you who dwell in the heav'ns; my eyes, my eyes, like the

hand___ of her mis- tress, so our eyes, our eyes are on the

filled___ with con - tempt. In - deed all too full is our soul with the

Ah...   Ah...

eyes___ of slaves on the hand, the hand of their lords.

Lord___ our God till he show us his mer-cy.

scorn___ of the rich, the dis - dain, the dis - dain of the proud.

Ah... Ah...

Solo top line in verses 1 & 3

mp

51

Our

Our eyes are on the Lord____ till he

Our

Our eyes are on the Lord____ till he

show____ us his mer - cy.

show____ us his mer - cy, till he show____ us his mer - cy.

Lord, You Are Good And Forgiving

Psalm 86

Stephen Dean

full   of love   to all   who   call.   call.

full   of love   to all   who   call.   call.

call.

call.

54

VERSES: *Cantor/Choir*

1. You, O Lord,___ are kind___ and quick___ to for - give, you hear us
2. All the na - tions come___ to you___ and a - dore, and praise your
3. God of all___ com - pas - sion, God___ of all love, whose pa - tience

when we call.___ Give heed, O Lord,___ give heed, O Lord,___ to my
ho - ly name.___ For you are great___ and you do mar - vel-lous
knows no end,___ O turn to me,___ O fount of lov - ing and

prayer, for I raise my voice to you.___
things, tru - ly you a - lone are God.___
truth, O take pit - y, Lord, on me.___

D.S.

55

Fill Us, Lord, With Your Love

Psalm 90

Christopher Walker

VERSES: *Unison choir*

1. Make us know the short-ness of our life that we learn
2. In the morn - ing fill us with your love, songs of glad-ness
3. Let your serv - ants see your might - y deeds. On our chil-dren

57

wis - dom of heart. Lord, re - lent! Is your an - ger for ev - er?
fill - ing all our days. Give us joy to out - weigh all the sad - ness
let your glo - ry shine. Lord our God, let your bless - ing be on us.

wis - dom of heart.
fill - ing all our days.
let your glo - ry shine.

Give to us your mer - cy from a - bove.
through the years, that we were far from you.
Give suc - cess to ev' - ry - thing we do.

Give to us your mer - cy from a - bove.
through the years, that we were far from you.
Give suc - cess to ev' - ry - thing we do.

Taste And See

Psalm 34

Christopher Walker

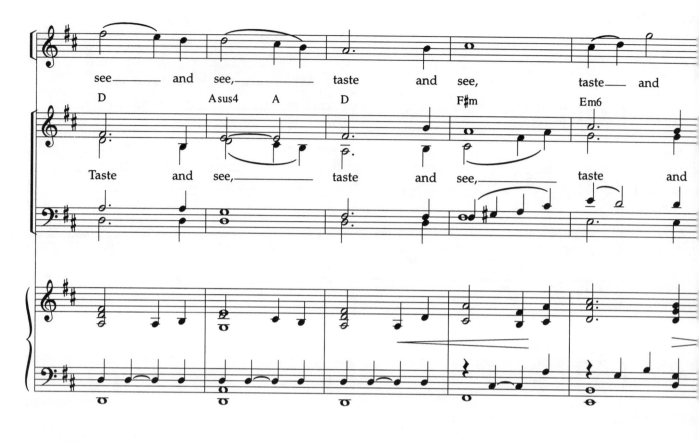

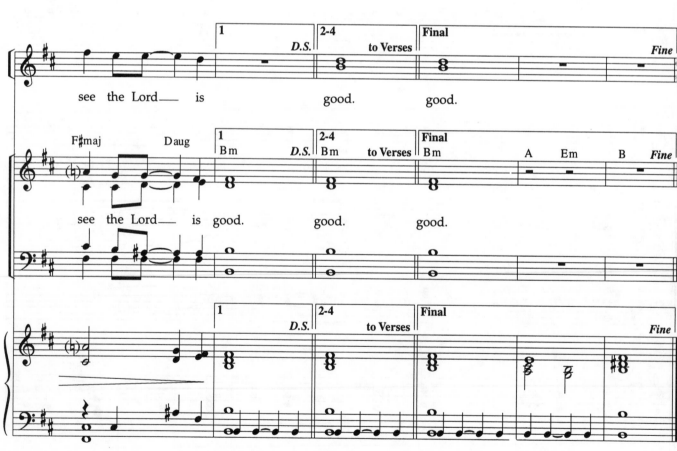

1. I will bless the Lord at all times, praises always on my lips. In the Lord my soul shall make its boast, the humble will rejoice at his call.
2. Glorify the Lord with me, together let us praise his name. I sought the Lord and he answered me, from all my terrors the Lord set me free.
3. Look towards the Lord, be radiant; never need you be ashamed. The helpless call, the Lord hears their cry and rescues them from all their distress.

For You My Soul Is Thirsting

Psalm 63

Anthony Hemson

All: For

God.

VERSES 1, 2, 4: *Cantor/Choir*

1. O God, you are — my God, for you — I long; — for —
2. So I gaze on you in the sanc-tu-'ry — to see — your —
4. For you have been — my help; in — the sha-dow of your

you my soul is thirst-ing. My — bod-y pines — for you like a
strength — and your glo-ry. For your love is bet-ter than life, my —
wings — I re-joice. My — soul — clings — to you; your —

VERSE 3: *Cantor/Choir*

dry,   wea - ry   land   with - out   wa - ter.
lips   will   speak   your   praise.
right   hand   holds   me   fast.

3. So I will bless you all— my life, in— your name I will lift— up my

hands.— My soul shall be filled as with a ban-quet. My— mouth shall

praise you with joy.

D.C.

64

I Lift Up My Eyes

Psalm 121

David Ogden

INTRO: Moderato (♩ = c.72)

REFRAIN: *1st time: Cantor/Choir; Repeat: All*

I lift up my eyes to the moun-

— tains:_____ from where_____ shall come my help? My help shall come from the

Lord, cre - a - tor of heav'n and earth. *All:* I earth. *Cantor/Choir:* I

Last time to CODA ⊕

D.S.

to Verses

VERSES: *Cantor/Choir*

lift up my eyes._____

1. The Lord will guard you and shade you;
2. The Lord will not let you fall.____

stand-ing at your right hand. By day the sun shall not harm you,____
God____ will guard your soul. Your go - ing out and your com-ing in

REFRAIN: *All*

nor shall the moon_____ at night._____
God will pro - tect_____ for ev - er.

I
I

D.S.

66

CODA:

Let The Lord Enter!

Psalm 24

Peter Ollis

He is the King____ of glo - ry.____ glo - ry.____ glo - ry.____
seek____ the face____ of God.____ God.____ God.____

VERSES: *Cantor/Choir*

1. God owns this plan - et and all its rich - es.____ The earth and____ ev - 'ry

2. Who is fit____ to climb God's moun - tain____ and stand____ in his

3. God____ will bless them,____ their sav - iour

mf

crea - ture___ be - longs___ to God.
God set the land on

ho - ly place?
Who- ev - er has in -

will bring jus - tice.
These peo - ple long to see the

top of the seas and an - chored it in the deep.___

D.S.

teg - ri - ty:___ not chas - ing sha - dows, not liv - ing lies.

D.S.

Lord,___ they seek the face___ of Ja - cob's God.

D.S.

dim.

D.S.

Guard My Soul

Psalm 131

Alan Smith

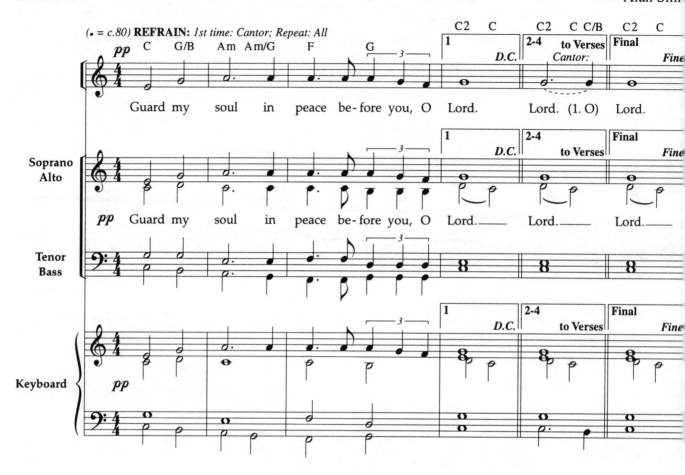

VERSE 1: *Cantor*

things— too great nor af - ter mar- vels be-yond me.

VERSE 2: *Cantor*

2. Tru - ly I have set my soul in si - lence and peace. As a weaned child on its

moth - er's breast, e - ven so is my soul.—

VERSE 3: *Cantor*

3. Is - rael, hope in the Lord both now and— for ev - er.

71

The Queen Stands At Your Right Hand

Psalm 45

Elizabeth Ree

ces - tral home. So will the king de - sire your beau - ty. He is your gold. She is led to the king with her com - pan - ions; they— jewels set in gold. Through my song may your name— be re - mem - bered. We will mas - ter, pay hom - age to him.

REFRAIN: *All* D.S.
The
Be - en - ter the pal - ace of the king.

REFRAIN: *All* D.S.
The praise you from age to age.

REFRAIN: *All* D.S.
The

D.S.

O God, You Search Me

Psalm 139

Bernadette Farrell

Verse text:

1. O God, you search me and you know me. All my thoughts lie o-pen to your gaze. When I walk or lie down you are be-

2. You know my rest-ing and my ris-ing. You dis-cern my pur-pose from a-far. And with love ev-er-last-ing you be-

3. Be-fore a word is on my tongue, Lord, you have known its mean-ing through and through. You are with me be-yond my un-der-

VERSE 4: *(a cappella, guitars tacent)*

4. Al - though your Spir-it is up - on— me, still I search— for shel - ter from your light.——

There is no-where on earth I can es - cape you:— e - ven the dark-ness is ra-diant in your sight.

VERSE 5:

5. For you cre-at-ed me and shaped me,—— gave me life—— with-in my moth-er's womb.——

For the won-der of who I am I praise you:—— safe in your hands, all cre-a-tion is made new.

Guard My Soul

C INSTRUMENT I

Alan Smith

C INSTRUMENT II

Alan Smith

Here I Am

C INSTRUMENT I

David Ogden

C INSTRUMENT II

David Ogden

Laudate Dominum

FLUTE · Jacques Berthier

OBOE · Jacques Berthier

B♭ TRUMPET · Jacques Berthier

(Chorale)

Teach Me, O God

C INSTRUMENT

Christopher Walker

It Is Good To Give Thanks

FLUTE

Stephen Dean

De Profundis Blues

Paul Wellicome

FLUTE

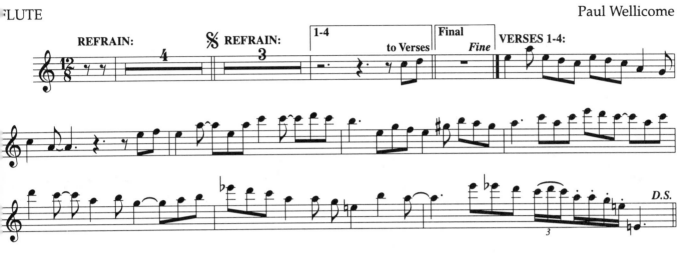

Fill Us, Lord, With Your Love

Christopher Walker

C INSTRUMENT

Bb INSTRUMENT

Christopher Walker

Your Love Is Finer Than Life

FLUTES I & II

Marty Haugen

Lord, You Are Good And Forgiving

C INSTRUMENT

Stephen Dean

B♭ INSTRUMENT

Stephen Dean

Taste And See

C INSTRUMENT

Christopher Walker

B♭ INSTRUMENT

Christopher Walker

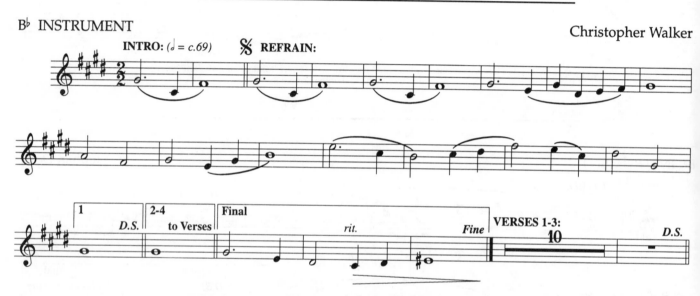

Canticle of Daniel

C INSTRUMENTS I & II

Christopher Walker

84

I Lift Up My Eyes

David Ogden

FLUTE

VIOLIN

David Ogden

Good People Are A Light

C INSTRUMENT

Paul Inwood

O God, You Search Me

OBOE

Bernadette Farrell

FRENCH HORN

Bernadette Farrell

Refrains

For permission to photocopy, see page 2.

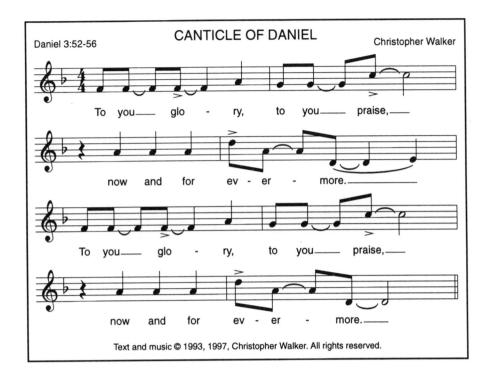

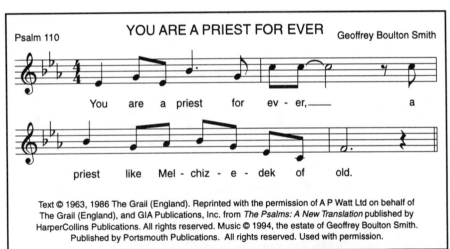

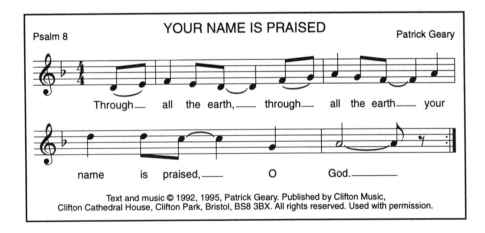

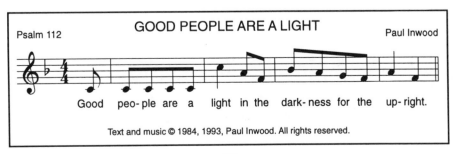

HERE I AM

Psalm 25

David Ogden

Here I am, here I am, I come to do your will, Lord, I have heard your call. Here I am, here I am, I come to do your will, Lord, your love is in my heart.

O LORD, BE MY HELP

Psalm 71

David Ogden

O— Lord, be my help, be the rock where I hide, be my tower of strength each day. O— Lord, be my hope, be the One whom I trust, be the Sav - iour who guides my way.

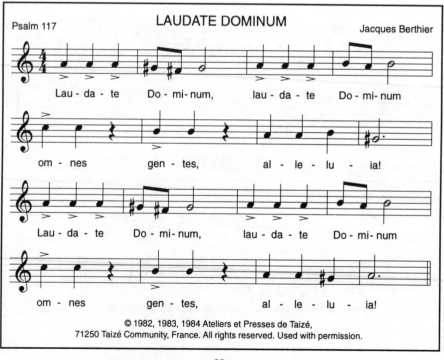

LAUDATE DOMINUM

Psalm 117

Jacques Berthier

Lau - da - te Do - mi - num, lau - da - te Do - mi - num om - nes gen - tes, al - le - lu - ia! Lau - da - te Do - mi - num, lau - da - te Do - mi - num om - nes gen - tes, al - le - lu - ia!

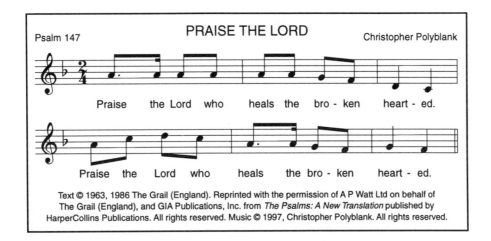

PRAISE THE LORD

Psalm 147 · Christopher Polyblank

Praise the Lord who heals the bro-ken heart-ed.

Praise the Lord who heals the bro-ken heart-ed.

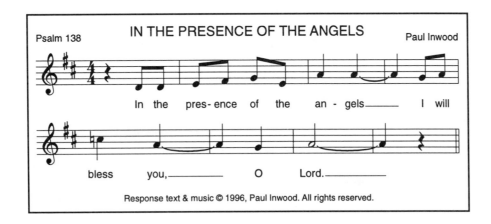

IN THE PRESENCE OF THE ANGELS

Psalm 138 · Paul Inwood

In the pres-ence of the an-gels____ I will

bless you,____ O Lord.____

TEACH ME, O GOD

Psalm 119 · Christopher Walker

Teach me, O God, to fol-low your ways, to

fol-low your ways to the end.____ My heart de-lights to

fol-low your ways, to fol-low your ways to the end.

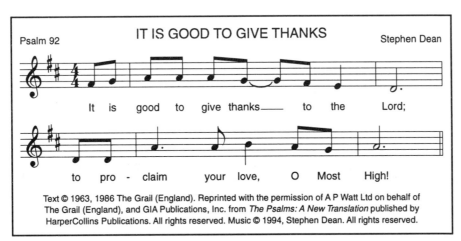

IT IS GOOD TO GIVE THANKS

Psalm 92 · Stephen Dean

It is good to give thanks____ to the Lord;

to pro-claim your love, O Most High!

For permission to photocopy, see page 2.

Psalm 50

I WILL SHOW GOD'S SALVATION

Stephen Dean

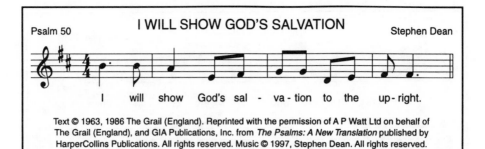

I will show God's sal - va - tion to the up - right.

Psalm 130

DE PROFUNDIS BLUES

Paul Wellicome

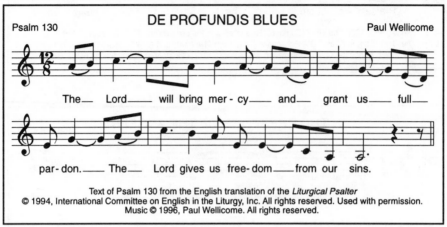

The— Lord— will bring mer - cy— and— grant us— full— par - don.— The— Lord gives us free-dom— from our sins.

Psalm 63

YOUR LOVE IS FINER THAN LIFE

Marty Haugen

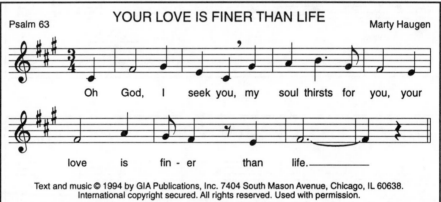

Oh God, I seek you, my soul thirsts for you, your love is fin - er than life.

Psalm 63

FOR YOU MY SOUL IS THIRSTING

Anthony Hemson

For you my soul is thirst-ing, O God, my God; O God, my God. For you my soul is thirst-ing, O God, my God.

Psalm 90

FILL US, LORD, WITH YOUR LOVE

Christopher Walker

Fill us, Lord, with your love. All our life we will sing and be glad. Fill us with your love. Fill us with your love.

For permission to photocopy, see page 2.

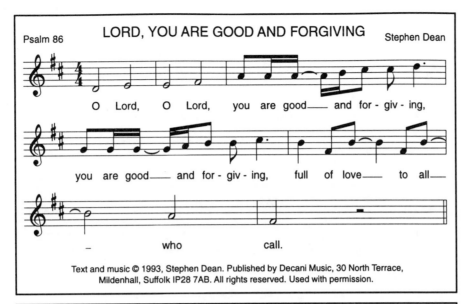

Psalm 86 — **LORD, YOU ARE GOOD AND FORGIVING** — Stephen Dean

O Lord, O Lord, you are good and for-giv-ing, you are good and for-giv-ing, full of love to all who call.

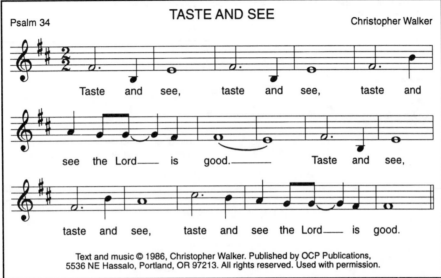

Psalm 34 — **TASTE AND SEE** — Christopher Walker

Taste and see, taste and see, taste and see the Lord is good. Taste and see, taste and see, taste and see the Lord is good.

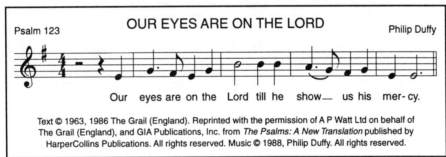

Psalm 123 — **OUR EYES ARE ON THE LORD** — Philip Duffy

Our eyes are on the Lord till he show us his mer-cy.

Psalm 121 — **I LIFT UP MY EYES** — David Ogden

I lift up my eyes to the moun-tains: from where shall come my help? My help shall come from the Lord, cre-a-tor of heav'n and earth.

For permission to photocopy, see page 2.

Psalm 24

LET THE LORD ENTER!

Peter Ollis

1. Let the Lord en - ter! He is the King—— of glo - ry.——
2. *These are the ones who seek—— the face—— of God.——*

Text of Psalm 24 from the English translation of the *Liturgical Psalter*

Psalm 131

GUARD MY SOUL

Alan Smith

Guard my soul in peace be - fore you, O Lord.

THE QUEEN STANDS AT YOUR RIGHT HAND

Psalm 45

Elizabeth Rees

1. The queen—— stands at your right hand, ar- rayed in—— gold.
2. *Be - hold the hand-maid of the Lord.—— Your will be done.*

Psalm 139

O GOD, YOU SEARCH ME

Bernadette Farrell

1. O God, you search me and you know me.
2. You know my rest - ing and my ris - ing.
3. Be - fore a word is on my tongue, Lord,
4. Al - though your Spir - it is up - on me,
5. For you cre - at - ed me and shaped me,

1. All my thoughts lie o - pen to your gaze.
2. You dis - cern my pur - pose from a - far.
3. you have known its mean - ing through and through.
4. still I search for shel - ter from your light.
5. gave me life with - in my moth - er's womb.

1. When I walk or lie down you are be - fore me:
2. And with love ev - er - last - ing you be - siege me:
3. You are with me be - yond my un - der - stand - ing:
4. There is no - where on earth I can es - cape you:
5. For the won - der of who I am I praise you:

1. ev - er the mak - er and keep - er of my days.
2. in ev - 'ry mo - ment of life or death, you are.
3. God of my pres - ent, my past and fu - ture, too.
4. e - ven the dark - ness is ra - diant in your sight.
5. safe in your hands, all cre - a - tion is made new.

For permission to photocopy, see page 2.

Topical Index

Common Psalms

Roman Lectionary

Liturgical Index

(Revised Common Lectionary)

Liturgical Index
(Roman Lectionary)